Condition of vegetation communities in Fort Necessity National Battlefield and Friendship Hill National Historic Site:

Eastern Rivers and Mountains Network summary report 2007–2009

Natural Resource Data Series NPS/ERMN/NRDS—2010/035

Stephanie J. Perles, Kristina K. Callahan, and Matthew R. Marshall

National Park Service
Northeast Region
Eastern Rivers and Mountains Network
Forest Resources Building
University Park, Pennsylvania 16802

March 2010

U.S. Department of the Interior
National Park Service
Natural Resource Program Center
Fort Collins, Colorado

The National Park Service, Natural Resource Program Center publishes a range of reports that address natural resource topics of interest and applicability to a broad audience in the National Park Service and others in natural resource management, including scientists, conservation and environmental constituencies, and the public.

The Natural Resource Data Series is intended for timely release of basic data sets and data summaries. Care has been taken to assure accuracy of raw data values, but a thorough analysis and interpretation of the data has not been completed. Consequently, the initial analyses of data in this report are provisional and subject to change.

All manuscripts in the series receive the appropriate level of peer review to ensure that the information is scientifically credible, technically accurate, appropriately written for the intended audience, and designed and published in a professional manner. Data in this report were collected and analyzed using methods based on established, peer-reviewed protocols and were analyzed and interpreted within the guidelines of the protocols.

Views, statements, findings, conclusions, recommendations, and data in this report are those of the author(s) and do not necessarily reflect views and policies of the National Park Service, U.S. Department of the Interior. Mention of trade names or commercial products does not constitute endorsement or recommendation for use by the National Park Service.

This report is available from the Eastern Rivers and Mountains Network website (http://science.nature.nps.gov/im/units/ERMN) and the Natural Resource Publications Management website (http://www.nature.nps.gov/publications/NRPM).

Please cite this publication as:

Perles, S. J., K. K. Callahan, and M. R. Marshall. 2010. Condition of vegetation communities in Fort Necessity National Battlefield and Friendship Hill National Historic Site: Eastern Rivers and Mountains Network summary report 2007–2009. Natural Resource Data Series NPS/ERMN/NRDS—2010/035. National Park Service, Fort Collins, Colorado.

NPS 336/101589, 476/101589, March 2010

Contents

Page

Figures iv

Tables v

Appendixes v

Executive Summary vi

Introduction 1

Methods 3

    Site Selection 3

    Field Methods 6

    Data Analysis 6

Results 7

    Stand Structure and Succession 7

    Forest Composition and Structure 7

    Forest Regeneration 11

    Forest Health 12

    Snags 12

    Coarse Woody Debris 13

    Shrubs 13

    Groundstory Diversity and Nativity 13

    Deer Browse Indicators 15

    Habitat Diversity 15

    Invasive Exotic Plant Species 16

    Early Detection of Exotic Invasive Plants and Animals 16

Discussion 17

Literature Cited 19

Figures

Page

Figure 1. Location of vegetation monitoring plots (2007–2009) in Fort Necessity National Battlefield..4

Figure 2. Location of vegetation monitoring plots (2007–2009) in Friendship Hill National Historic Site..5

Figure 3. Plot design for the Eastern Rivers and Mountains Network Vegetation Monitoring protocol...6

Figure 4. The average relative density of select species for canopy trees, saplings, and seedlings in the oak/tuliptree-dominated forest in Fort Necessity National Battlefield (FONE [n=9])...8

Figure 5. The average relative density of select species for canopy trees, saplings, and seedlings in the successional forest in Fort Necessity National Battlefield (FONE [n=4]). 9

Tables

Page

Table 1. Distribution of plots in stand structural classes from monitoring plots visited between 2007 and 2009 in Fort Necessity National Battlefield (FONE) and Friendship Hill National Historic Site (FRHI)... 7

Table 2. Percentage of plots with adequate tree regeneration in Fort Necessity National Battlefield (FONE) and Friendship Hill National Historic Site (FRHI) at two levels of browse intensity.. 11

Table 3. Summary data on snags in Fort Necessity National Battlefield (FONE) and Friendship Hill National Historic Site (FRHI).. 12

Table 4. Average percent cover and number of stems per microplot for the most abundant shrub species in monitoring plots in Fort Necessity National Battlefield (FONE [n=15]). 14

Table 5. Average percent cover and number of stems per microplot for the most abundant shrub species in monitoring plots in Friendship Hill National Historic Site (FRHI [n=15]).. 14

Table 6. Average plot and quadrat species richness in Fort Necessity National Battlefield (FONE) and Friendship Hill National Historic Site (FRHI)...................... 14

Table 7. Average values for percent of total quadrat cover and species richness of nonnative and native species calculated from monitoring plots in Fort Necessity National Battlefield (FONE) and Friendship Hill National Historic Site (FRHI). 14

Table 8. Number of monitoring plots in which invasive exotic plant species were observed in Fort Necessity National Battlefield (FONE) and Friendship Hill National Historic Site (FRHI) between 2007–2009.. 15

Appendixes

Page

Appendix A. Plants observed in Fort Necessity National Battlefield during vegetation monitoring plot sampling, 2007–2009. 23

Appendix B. Plants observed in Friendship Hill National Historic Site during vegetation monitoring plot sampling, 2007–2009. 29

Executive Summary

Beginning in 2007, the Eastern Rivers and Mountains Network (ERMN) of the National Park Service (NPS) began monitoring vegetation communities and soil in eight of its nine parks. The objective of this monitoring program is to provide information on the condition of the parks' vegetation and soil and how this condition is changing through time. Permanent long-term monitoring plots have been established in Fort Necessity National Battlefield (FONE, 15 plots) and Friendship Hill National Historic Site (FRHI, 15 plots). Within the permanent plots, data are collected on forest stand structure; tree health, growth, and mortality; tree regeneration; coarse woody debris; shrubs; groundstory diversity; invasive species; and soil. The last panel of plots will be established in 2010, and in 2011 the first panel of plots will be revisited, providing data on how vegetation is changing through time.

This report summarizes vegetation monitoring data collected between 2007 and 2009 in FONE and FRHI and presents the condition of the parks' vegetation based on those data. These data provide a snap-shot of the status of the vegetation communities and are compared to expected ranges of variability for eastern forests. The results reported here provide highlights of the available data but additional measures are being investigated and may be reported in the future.

Vegetation condition highlights within FONE and FRHI include:

- Forest stands within FONE are predominately mature, while forest stands in FRHI are typically young, with fewer mature stands.

- In oak- and tuliptree-dominated forests in FONE, trees that are regenerating (trees of the future) are not the same species as are present in the canopy (present trees). Oaks and tuliptrees comprise a significant portion of the canopy trees; however, they are underrepresented in the sapling and seedling layers. In contrast; maple species comprise a much larger portion of the seedling layer than the canopy. Given these distributions, the parks' dry forests will contain fewer oak and tuliptrees and more maples as these forests mature.

- In FRHI, between 25–50% of the plots contain sufficient tree regeneration, depending on the browse intensity. If browse pressure is low in FONE the vast majority of stands contain sufficient seedlings and saplings to regenerate the canopy. However, under high browse intensity only half of the plots in FONE contain insufficient tree regeneration.

- In general, select herbaceous plant species that are considered sensitive to deer browse are less common in FONE and FRHI than in other ERMN parks. No indicator species were found in more than one third of the plots in FONE or FRHI.

- Very few occurrences of forest pests and pathogens were detected in the monitoring plots, which may indicate that these pests and pathogens are rare or absent within the parks.

- Snag (standing dead trees) densities and the volume of coarse woody debris (fallen logs) within the two parks are typical of values found in other second-growth forests in the eastern United States. Snags and coarse woody debris provide important habitat for wildlife. FONE tends to have fewer snags, especially large snags, than FRHI.

- The shrubs layer in both parks is characterized by a mixture of native and exotic invasive species. Common native shrubs include: blackberries, blueberries, spicebush, and viburnums. Morrow's honeysuckle, multiflora rosa, Japanese barberry, and autumn olive are the most abundant exotic invasive shrub species.

- The oak- and tuliptree-dominated forest in the southwestern section of FONE's Main Unit contains the most diverse groundstory, as well as the highest percentage of native species cover and richness. The groundstory in the successional forests in FONE and all forests in FRHI were less diverse, and the percent cover and richness of nonnative species was much higher.

- Invasive exotic species were found in 73% of plots in FONE and 80% of plots in FRHI. The most commonly observed invasive exotic plant species in both parks was multiflora rose. One early detection of privet, an exotic invasive species new to FRHI, was documented by the vegetation monitoring field crew in 2008 in FRHI.

In general, forests in FONE and FRHI are typical of other second-growth forests in the Appalachian Mountains; however, results from the monitoring data underscore two important points for park managers:

1) **Invasive exotic plant species are a pervasive and spreading threat to the parks' vegetation communities.** This finding underscores the vital importance of the many ongoing projects in FONE and FRHI directed by park managers, the Southern Laurel Highlands Plant Management Partnership, and external researchers that are addressing invasive exotic plants. When possible, additional resources should be strategically allocated to managing invasive exotic species by:
   a) removing invasive exotic plants from areas in which these species are less abundant.
   b) detecting and eliminating (when possible) new populations of invasive exotic species novel to the parks (implementation of the Early Detection and Rapid Response protocol).
   c) working with partners to acquire and release approved biological controls for invasive exotic species that are widespread and abundant in the parks.

2) **The factors contributing to poor tree regeneration, particularly of oaks, need to be investigated further in order to evaluate potential management actions.** This regeneration failure could be attributed to one or more of the following factors: dense shade from canopy or subcanopy trees; competition from shrubs, ferns, or grasses; altered disturbance regimes, including fire suppression; browse pressure from white-tailed deer; and/or soil infertility. As more data on both vegetation and soil are collected from the monitoring plots we will investigate correlations between these factors discussed and tree regeneration in FONE and FRHI. We hope to be able to provide guidance on potential management actions pertaining to forest regeneration.

Introduction

In 2007, the Eastern Rivers and Mountains Network (ERMN) of the National Park Service (NPS) began monitoring vegetation communities and soil in eight of its nine parks. This monitoring effort is a component of the ERMN Vital Signs monitoring program (Marshall and Piekielek 2007) as part of the nationwide NPS Inventory and Monitoring Program (Fancy et al. 2009).

Long-term monitoring of vegetation and soils was identified among the highest priority vital signs during the ERMN prioritization process (Marshall and Piekielek 2007). The vital sign process highlighted the importance of plant species diversity and functional plant communities as natural resources critical to the parks. These vegetation communities also serve as an integrated measure of terrestrial ecosystem health by expressing information about climate, soils, and disturbance. Furthermore, vegetation serves as a base for other trophic components such as wildlife.

The ERMN Vegetation and Soil Monitoring Program provides information regarding the condition of the parks' vegetation and soil and how this condition is changing through time. Data generated by this program contribute to the monitoring of several of the network's vital signs, including: Forest, Woodland, Shrubland, and Riparian Plant Communities; Status and Trends of Invasive/Exotic Plants, Animals, and Diseases; Early Detection of Invasive/Exotic Plants, Animals, and Diseases; and Soil Function and Dynamics.

Numerous ecological and anthropogenic forces affect the parks' vegetation. Ecological factors such as geology, soil nutrient availability, weather, and disturbance patterns directly influence the structure, composition, and dynamics of the vegetation. Some anthropogenic stressors are easily identified, such as visitor overuse or loss and fragmentation of habitat due to development inside and outside of the parks. Many changes in forest vegetation through time are often linked to several interacting ecological and anthropogenic factors. Exotic species, white-tailed deer (*Odocoileus virginianus*), atmospheric acid and nutrient deposition, climate change, altered disturbance regimes, and changes in land use are also important factors affecting the parks' vegetation (Rentch 2006, Perles et al. 2009).

Depending on successional stage, disturbance history, and site conditions, there are certain parameters within which a terrestrial vegetation ecosystem can be described as "healthy" (Tierney et al 2009). By measuring taxonomic, structural, and demographic features an assessment can be made as to whether or not the ecosystem's parameters fall within expected or accepted norms and ranges of variability. These measures serve as indicators of ecological integrity that can be explicitly linked to park management.

This report is intended to provide preliminary results to natural resource managers at Fort Necessity National Battlefield (FONE) and Friendship Hill National Historic Site (FRHI) on the condition of the vegetation communities in the parks utilizing the first three years of collected data. These data provide a snap-shot of the status of the vegetation communities and are compared to expected ranges of variability for eastern forests. In the future, when monitoring plots have been revisited, data will be available on how vegetation is changing through time and these results will also be presented.

Methods

Although a brief overview of the vegetation and soil monitoring methods is provided here, a detailed rationale of the sampling design and methods, in addition to Standard Operating Procedures, is provided in the Vegetation and Soil Monitoring Protocol (Perles et al. 2009). The protocol was based on the U.S. Forest Service (USFS) Forest Inventory and Analysis (FIA) program (USFS 2007) and the vegetation monitoring protocols of four other Inventory and Monitoring programs in the eastern United States (Sanders et al. 2006, Schmit et al. 2006, Tierney and Faber-Langendoen 2007, Comisky et al. 2009). Adopting widely used protocols facilitates comparisons of ERMN data with other NPS networks and regional data sets.

Site Selection

Vegetation and soil are monitored at permanent plots, since the use of permanent plots increases power to detect trends through time. For each park, a regular grid of potential plot locations was overlain on the park, with plot locations within the grid located 250 m apart. Plots that fell on steep slopes (>56%) and non-vegetated or intensively managed lands were removed from the grid. Sampling locations were selected from the regular grid using a generalized random-tessellation stratified (GRTS) design (McDonald 2004, Stevens and Olsen 2004). The three main advantages to a GRTS design are: 1) the GRTS design is spatially balanced, wherein there is generally uniform dispersion of sampling sites over the area of interest; 2) the GRTS design allows for flexible sample size, such that sites can be added to or excluded from the sampling plan without compromising the integrity of the overall design; and 3) the GRTS method is a probabilistic sampling design, whereby sampling points are randomly chosen from among those in a systematic grid, eliminating site selection bias, and allowing inference to the entire sampling frame (Stevens and Olsen 2004).

Plots are sampled on a four-year panel design, in which one panel containing one-fourth of a park's total plots is sampled each year. On the fifth year, the first panel is re-sampled. Sampling began in both parks in 2007 and took place in May of 2007, and July of 2008 and 2009. Five plots have been established in each year in both parks, for a total of 15 plots per park thus far. The locations of the vegetation monitoring plots in FONE and FRHI are shown in Figures 1 and 2, respectively.

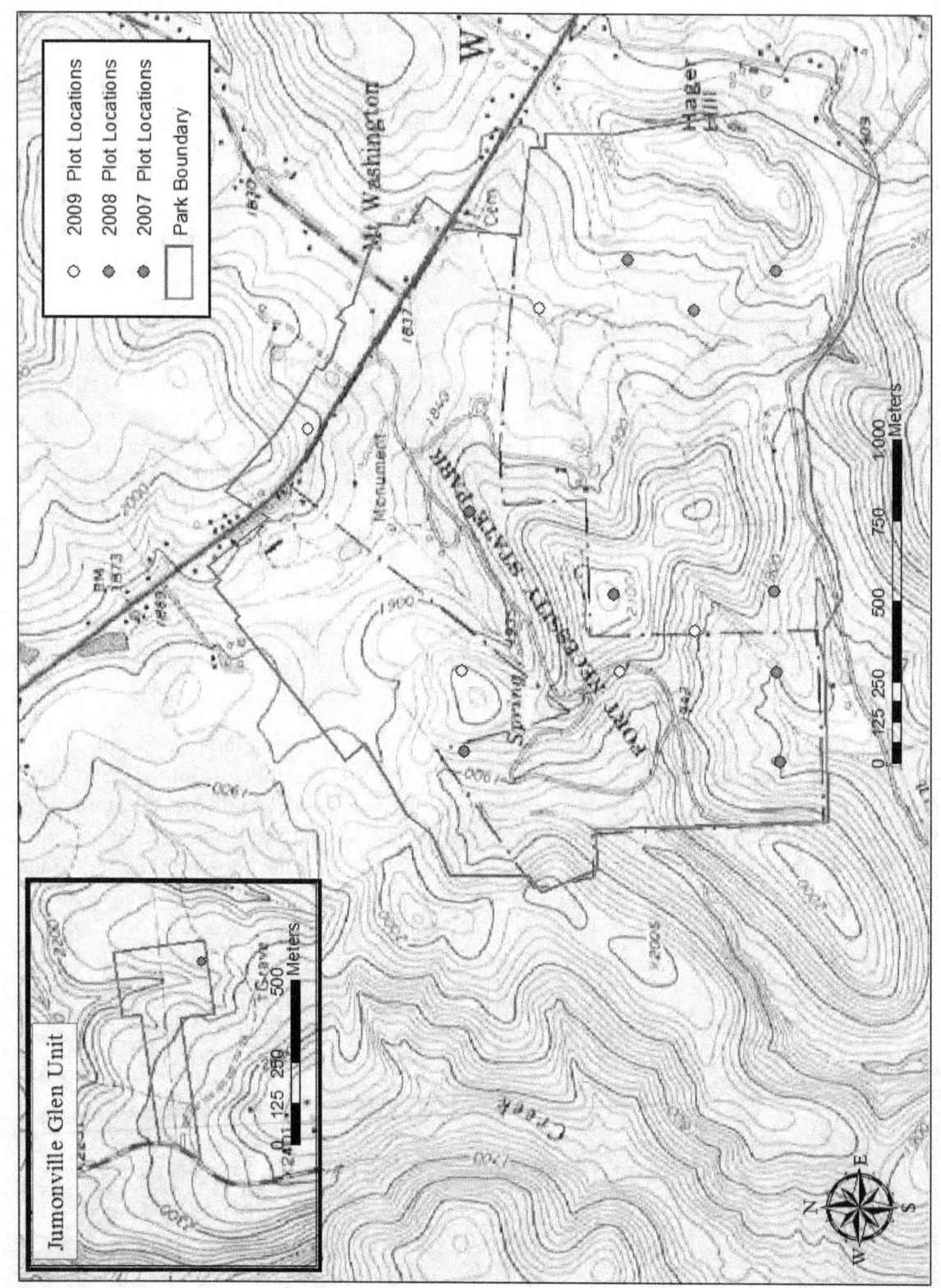

Figure 1. Location of vegetation monitoring plots (2007–2009) in Fort Necessity National Battlefield.

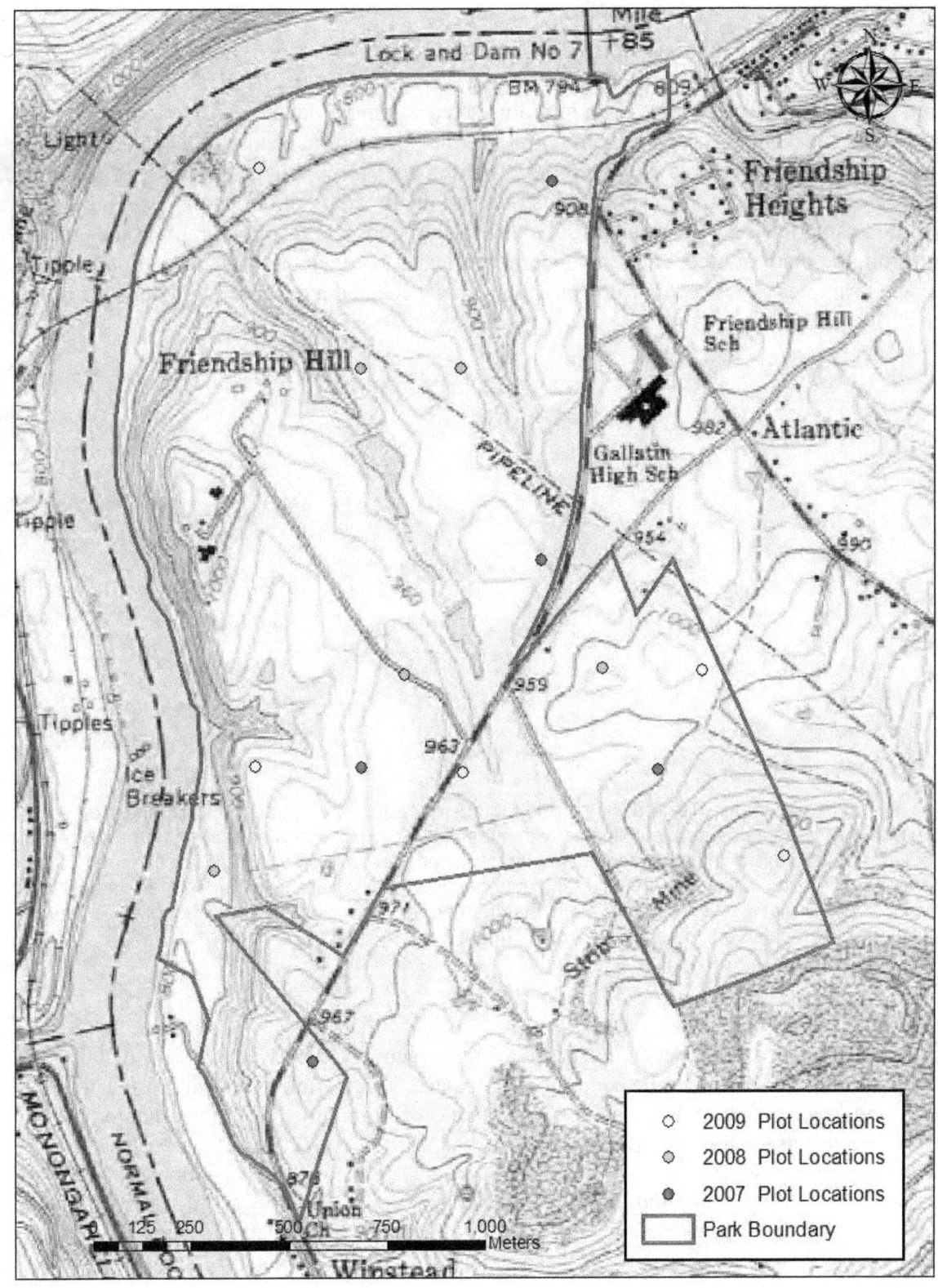

Figure 2. Location of vegetation monitoring plots (2007–2009) in Friendship Hill National Historic Site.

Field Methods

At each plot, ERMN monitors a suite of vegetation and soil variables. The plot design includes several embedded sampling units (Figure 3). Tree, stand, and site measurements are collected within fixed-area, circular plots, 15-m in radius. Tree regeneration and shrub measurements are collected on four 2-m radius circular microplots embedded within each plot. Data on coarse woody debris are collected using line intersect sampling (Van Wagner 1964) along six 15 meter transects. Data on understory plant composition and the diversity of understory species are monitored using twelve 1-m^2 quadrats set along the six transects. A photograph of the plot is taken from the plot's southern edge to document change in vegetation structure through time. Three soil samples are collected from sampling frames located adjacent to the plot's northern edge.

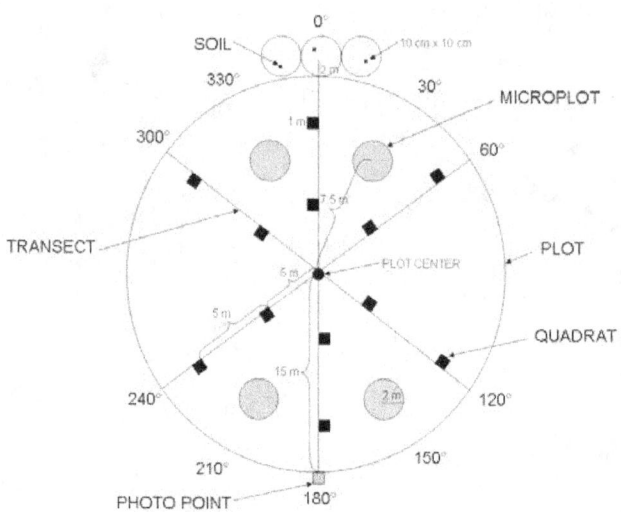

Figure 3. Plot design for the Eastern Rivers and Mountains Network Vegetation Monitoring protocol. Tree, stand, and site measurements are collected within the plot. Tree regeneration and shrub measurements are collected in the microplots. Data on coarse woody debris are collected along the transects. Data on understory plant composition and the diversity of understory species are collected in the quadrats. A photograph of the plot is taken from the plot's southern edge. Three soil samples are collected from sampling frames located adjacent to the plot's northern edge.

Data Analysis

This report summarizes the vegetation monitoring data collected between 2007 and 2009 in FONE and FRHI. We present the condition of the parks' vegetation based on those data. These data provide a snap-shot of the status of the vegetation communities and are compared to expected ranges of variability for eastern forests.

The results reported here are highlights of the available data but additional measures are being investigated and may be reported in the future. Furthermore, as plots are revisited through time and additional data are collected we will report how the conditions discussed below are changing through time.

Results

Stand Structure and Succession

The parks' vegetation is primarily forest, though the forest stands vary greatly in age and land use history. A wide variety of non-forested vegetation types also exist in the parks. Monitoring the successional stage of the vegetation plots provides a picture of the shifting mosaic of stand structures within the parks. Based on the monitoring plot data, forest stands within FONE are predominately mature, while forest stands in FRHI are typically young, with fewer mature stands (Table 1).

For each plot, the quadratic mean diameter (QMD) of the plot was calculated. The quadratic mean diameter is the "average" diameter for the plot; specifically, the diameter of a hypothetical tree with its basal area equal to the plot's average basal area of live trees (Curtis and Marshall 2000). The plots are then classified into non-forested, pole, mature, and late-successional categories based on the following classification (adapted from Frelich and Lorimer 1991): non-forested = no trees in the plot; pole = 10 cm≤QMD>26 cm; mature = 26 cm≤QMD>46 cm; late-successional = QMD≥46 cm dbh. Table 1 shows the percentage of plots that fall into these categories.

Forest Composition and Structure

The relative proportion of species among different strata of a forest stand provides information on the current and future composition of the forest. For this analysis, the relative density by species for trees, saplings, and seedlings were calculated for each park. These data provide an illustration of how the species composition shifts among the canopy, sapling, and seedling layers of the forest (Figures 4, 5, and 6).

Oak- and tuliptree-dominated forests in FONE (Figure 4) exhibit similar patterns of species distribution as those observed in xeric forests in other ERMN parks. Oak species (*Quercus* spp.) make up a significant portion of the canopy trees, around 30% of the standing live trees. However, oaks are underrepresented in the sapling layer (4% of saplings) and the seedling layer (5% of seedlings). In contrast, maple species (*Acer* spp.) comprise 30% of the canopy trees and 50% of the seedlings. [Interestingly, maple species are absent from the sapling layer in these FONE plots. In other ERMN parks, relative density of maples in the sapling layer is intermediate between that of the canopy and seedling layers.] In addition, tuliptree (*Liriodendron tulipifera*)

Table 1. Distribution of plots in stand structural classes from monitoring plots visited between 2007 and 2009 in Fort Necessity National Battlefield (FONE) and Friendship Hill National Historic Site (FRHI).

Stand structural class	FONE		FRHI	
	Number of plots (n=15)	Percent of total plots	Number of plots (n=15)	Percent of total plots
Non-forested	0	0%	0	0%
Pole	3	20%	8	53%
Mature	12	80%	6	40%
Late-successional	0	0%	1	7%

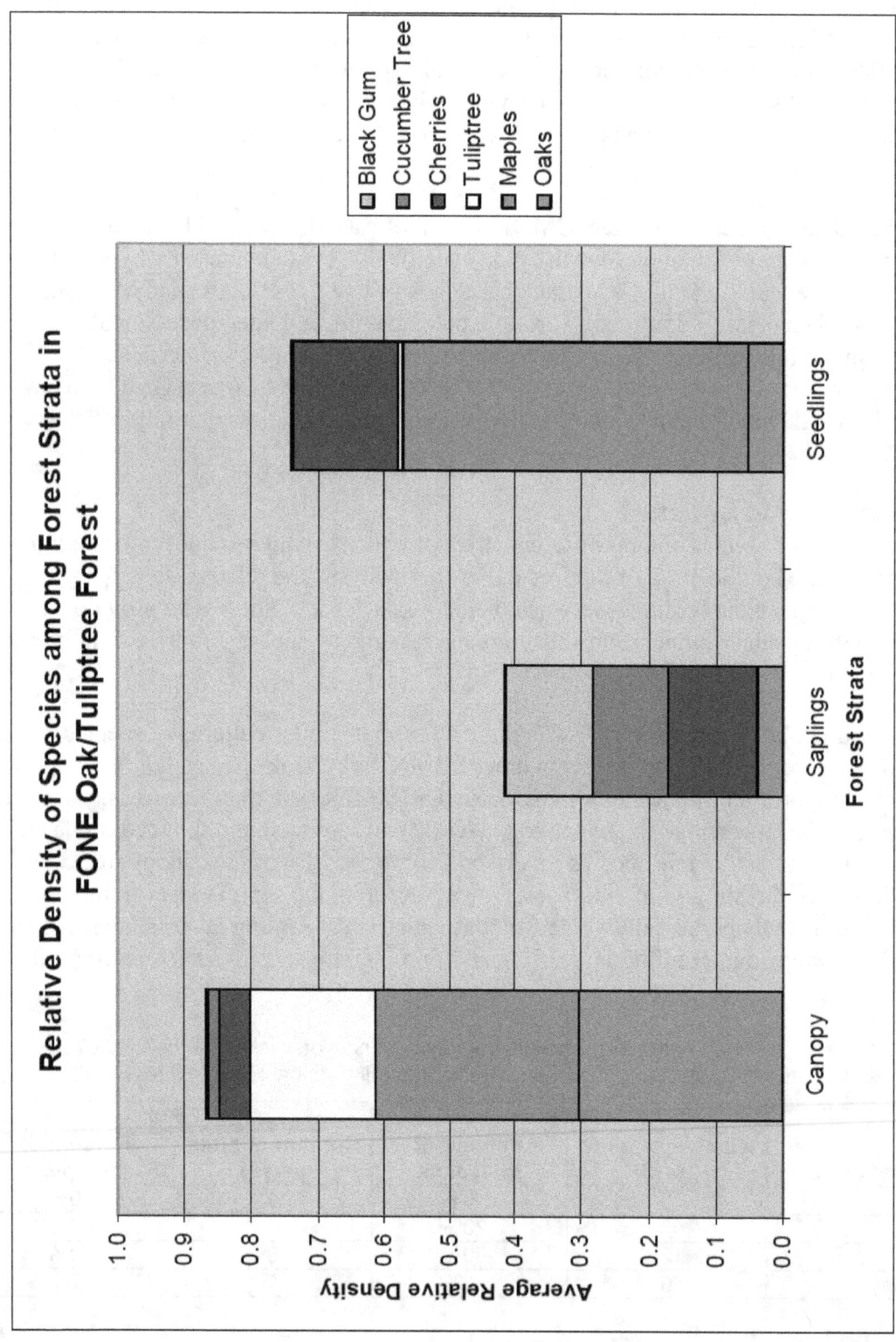

Figure 4. The average relative density of select species for canopy trees, saplings, and seedlings in the oak/tuliptree-dominated forest in Fort Necessity National Battlefield (FONE [n=9]).

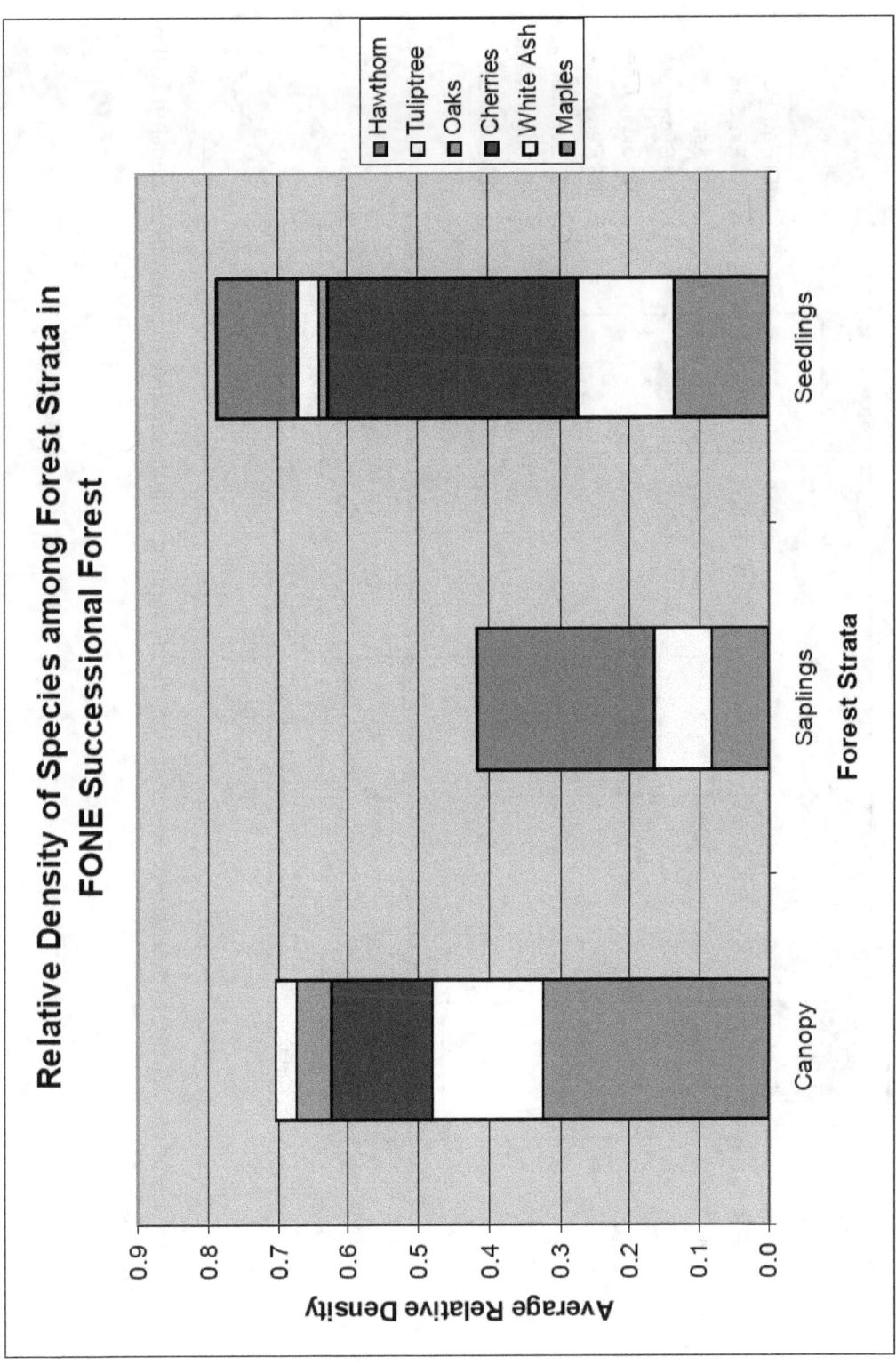

Figure 5. The average relative density of select species for canopy trees, saplings, and seedlings in the successional forest in Fort Necessity National Battlefield (FONE [n=4]).

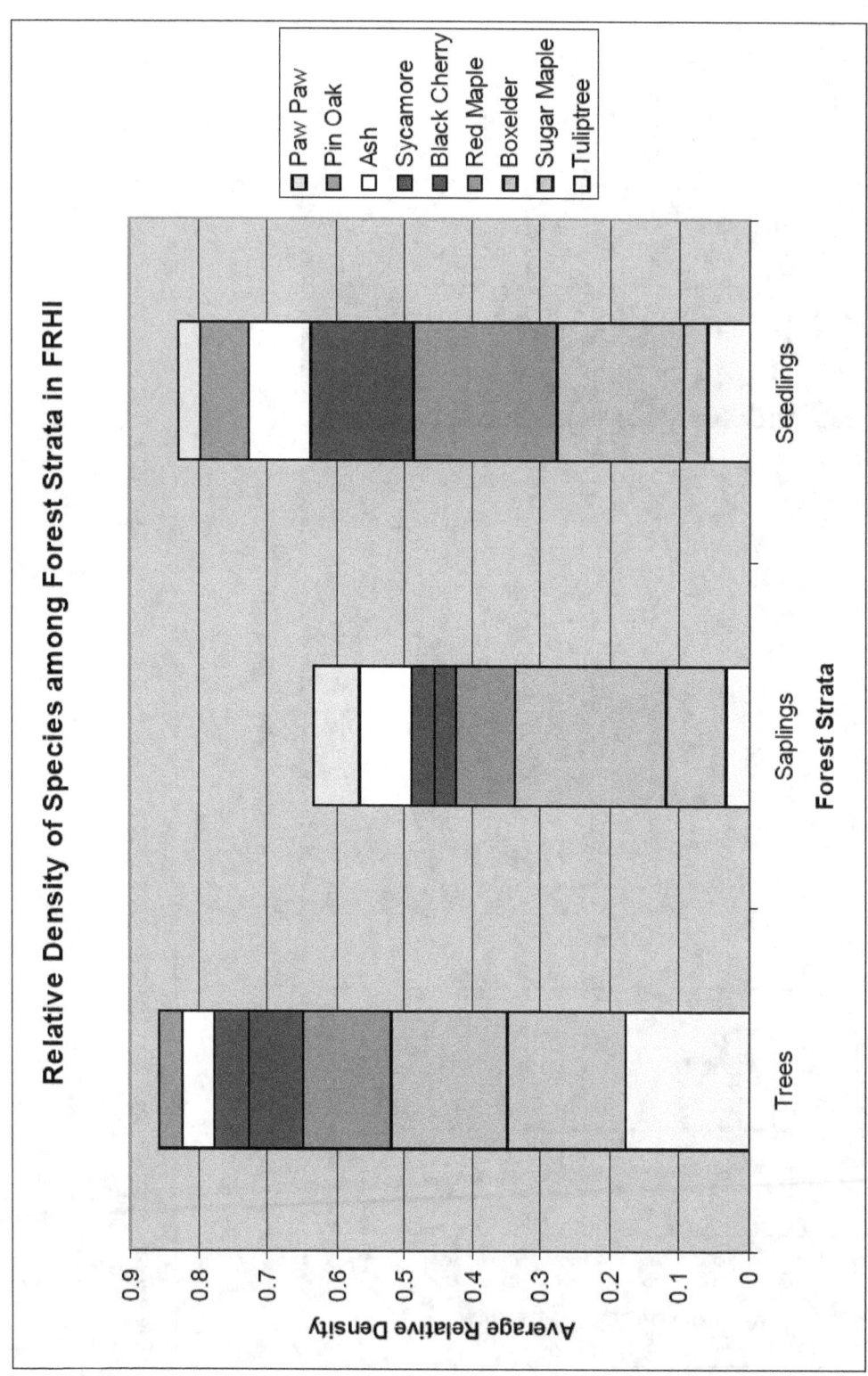

Figure 6. The average relative density of select species for canopy trees, saplings, and seedlings in forest of Friendship Hill National Historic Site (FRHI [n=15]).

is common in the canopy (19%, but rare to absent in the sapling and seedling layers (<1%). Given these species distributions, the park's dry forests will contain fewer oaks and tuliptrees, and more maples, predominantly red maple (*Acer rubrum*), as these forests mature in the future.

In successional forests in FONE (Figure 5), future canopy species composition will likely be similar to the current canopy composition, heavily dominated by maples and cherries (*Prunus* spp.). Tuliptree and white ash (*Fraxinus americana*) will also likely continue to persist in the forest. Due to their growth form and the dense shade from closed canopy stands, hawthorns (*Crataegus* spp.) will probably not comprise a significant proportion of the future canopy despite their current abundance in the sapling and seedlings layers.

In FRHI (Figure 6), species distribution across forest strata is somewhat uniform. In general, the canopy dominants are also well represented in the sapling and seedling layers, though tuliptree and sugar maple (*Acer saccharum*) are more abundant in the canopy and red maple and black cherry (*Prunus serotina*) are more abundant in the seedling layer. As would be expected from a pioneer species, sycamore (*Platanus occidentalis*) is not represented in the seedling layer since there is insufficient light on the forest floor for this species' seedlings to persist. Also, paw paw (*Asimina triloba*) is not represented in the canopy since this species rarely grows to attain canopy height.

Forest Regeneration

One approach to assessing forest regeneration quantifies whether current seedling quantities are sufficient to restock a forest stand's canopy trees. McWilliams et al. (2005) developed an index for hardwood stands in Pennsylvania that assigns point values to seedlings by size class and to saplings observed within the 2-m radius circular microplots. McWilliams et al. (2005) suggested that the standard guideline for acceptable regeneration is an index value of 25 per microplot in areas with low deer densities. In areas where high deer densities are likely to impact tree regeneration an acceptable index value is 100. A forest plot is considered adequately regenerated if at least 70% of the microplots (three out of the four microplots) exceed the stocking index (McWilliams et al. 2001).

Based on the results presented in Table 2, if browse pressure is low in FONE most stands contain sufficient seedlings and saplings to regenerate the canopy; however, under high browse intensity less than half of the plots in FONE contain insufficient tree regeneration. Compared to other ERMN parks, FONE contains the highest proportion of plots with sufficient regeneration at both levels of browse intensity.

Table 2. Percentage of plots with adequate tree regeneration in Fort Necessity National Battlefield (FONE) and Friendship Hill National Historic Site (FRHI) at two levels of browse intensity.

Browse intensity	FONE (n=15)	FRHI (n=15)
Low Browse Intensity (Index > 25)	86.7%	53.3%
High Browse Intensity (Index > 100)	46.7%	26.7%

Approximately 25 or 50% of plots in FRHI contain sufficient regeneration under high or low browse intensity, respectively. The percent of plots with sufficient regeneration under low browse pressure in FRHI is the lowest of any ERMN park. This regeneration failure could be due to one or more potentially interacting factors, including: dense shade from canopy or subcanopy trees; competition from shrubs, ferns, or grasses; stand age; browse pressure; and/or soil infertility. In the future, we hope to use the monitoring data to look for correlations between these factors and regeneration within the park.

Forest Health

No occurrences of forest pests and pathogens have been detected in the monitoring plots. This probably indicates that these pests and pathogens are rare or absent within the parks. For a complete list of the forest pests and pathogens targeted by this study, see the ERMN Vegetation and Soil Monitoring Protocol (Perles et al 2009).

The health of each tree in the monitoring plots is measured using standardized assessments of tree vigor and branch dieback (Perles et al 2009). These measurements were first collected in 2009. As additional data are collected, we will provide vigor estimates for individual tree species in the parks as well as trends in tree vigor.

Snags

Standing dead trees, or snags, are important structural features in forests and provide habitat for cavity-nesting birds and mammals. The density and size of snags are indicative of habitat availability for those species. Summary data on snags in FONE and FRHI are presented in Table 3. FONE tends to have fewer snags, especially large snags, than FRHI.

The values shown in Table 3 are typical of second-growth forests that are similar in age to those in the two parks. In a hemlock-northern hardwood stand in Pennsylvania standing snags accounted for 14% of the total basal area (6.7 m^2/ha) and 12% of the total stem density (49 snags/ha; Tritton and Siccama 1990). In mesic oak-hickory stands in Connecticut snags accounted for 5–15% of the total basal area (1.3–3.4 m^2/ha) and 8–19% of the total stem density (47–109 snags/ha; Tritton and Siccama 1990). In hardwood forests in West Virginia snag densities ranged from 22.4–55.1/ha (Carey 1983). In chestnut oak and oak-hickory stands in southwestern Virginia snag densities ranged from 62.2–69.2/ha (Rosenberg et al 1998).

Table 3. Summary data on snags in Fort Necessity National Battlefield (FONE) and Friendship Hill National Historic Site (FRHI).

All Snags	FONE (n=15)	FRHI (n=15)
Basal Area (m2/ha)	1.6	1.7
Percent of Total Tree Basal Area	4.9%	6.7%
Volume (m3/ha)	12.1	11.0
Percent of Total Tree Volume	3.8%	4.4%
Density (snags/ha)	46.2	64.1
Percent of Total Tree Density	8.7%	11.2%
Number of Live Trees / Snag	10	7
Large Snags (DBH > 30 cm)		
Density (large snags/ha)	4.7	5.6
Percent of Total Large Tree Density	5.8%	3.5%
Number of Live Trees / Snag	36	18

Old-growth forests also exhibit variability in snag densities ranging from 10–20 snags/ha in southern Appalachia (Runkle 1998, 2000), to 43 snags/ha in Kentucky (McComb and Muller 1983), and 39–73 snag/ha in northern Michigan and Wisconsin (Goodburn and Lorimer 1998).

Coarse Woody Debris

Fallen logs, or coarse woody debris, provide important habitat for microbes, arthropods, amphibians, reptiles, small mammals, and fungi. Among the 15 plots in FONE, the average coarse woody debris volume is 25.1 m^3/ha, which is 10.7% of the standing live tree volume on average. Among FRHI plots (n=15), average coarse woody debris volume is 28.0 m^3/ha, or 8.8% of the standing live tree volume on average.

Coarse woody debris volume can range from 25 m^3/ha in even-aged northern hardwood stands to 102 m^3/ha in old-growth northern hardwood forest in northern Michigan and Wisconsin (Goodburn and Lorimer 1998). Other published values include 46–132 m^3/ha for mixed oak forests (Harmon et al 1983) and 48 m^3/ha for old growth-forests in eastern Kentucky (Muller and Liu 1991), though the latter study only measured logs >20 cm in diameter.

Shrubs

The shrub layer in both parks is characterized by a mixture of native and exotic invasive species (Tables 4 and 5). In FONE, blackberries (*Rubus* spp.), blueberries (*Vaccinium* spp.), and viburnums (*Viburnum* spp.) are the most abundant native species, found primarily in the oak- and tuliptree-dominated forest in the southwestern section of the park's Main Unit. Morrow's honeysuckle (*Lonicera morrowii*), multiflora rose (*Rosa multiflora*), and Japanese barberry (*Berberis thunbergii*) are the most abundant exotic invasive species, common in successional forests and old fields. On average, microplots within monitoring plots contain 2.3 species in FONE.

In FRHI, the most abundant native shrub is spicebush (*Lindera benzoin*), followed by Allegheny blackberry (*Rubus alleghieniensis*) and viburnums (*Viburnum* spp.). Exotic invasive species such as multiflora rose (*Rosa multiflora*), autumn olive (*Elaeagnus umbellata*), and Morrow's honeysuckle (*Lonicera morrowii*) are also common in FRHI. On average, microplots within FRHI's monitoring plots contain 1.7 shrub species.

Groundstory Diversity and Nativity

The groundstory of most vegetation communities is the most diverse strata. Thus, diversity and nativity of this vegetation layer is an important component of the overall health of the vegetation community. Tables 6 and 7 show several metrics that will be monitored to determine trends in groundstory vegetation diversity and nativity in FONE and FRHI.

The oak- and tuliptree-dominated forest in the southwestern section of FONE's Main Unit contain the highest average plot and quadrat richness of any ERMN park, and the percentage of native species cover and richness is also generally high. The groundstory in the successional forests in FONE and all forests in FRHI were less diverse and the percent cover and richness of nonnative species was much higher (Table 8).

Table 4. Average percent cover and number of stems per microplot for the most abundant shrub species in monitoring plots in Fort Necessity National Battlefield (FONE [n=15]).

Shrub species	Percent cover	Number of stems
Bristly dewberry (*Rubus hispidus*)	4.4	13.2
Morrow's honeysuckle (*Lonicera morrowii*)	3.5	0.6
Multiflora rosa (*Rosa multiflora*)	2.2	2.0
Blue Ridge blueberry (*Vaccinium pallidum*)	2.0	2.6
Blueberry (*Vaccinium* sp.)	1.9	1.5
Japanese barberry (*Berberis thunbergii*)	1.5	1.0
Mapleleaf viburnum (*Viburnum acerifolium*)	0.6	1.5
Blackberry (*Rubus* sp.)	0.5	0.7
Allegheny blackberry (*Rubus allegheniensis*)	0.5	0.7
Deerberry (*Vaccinium stamineum*)	0.5	1.6
Southern arrowwod (*Viburnum dentatum*)	0.3	0.6

Table 5. Average percent cover and number of stems per microplot for the most abundant shrub species in monitoring plots in Friendship Hill National Historic Site (FRHI [n=15]).

Shrub species	Percent cover	Number of stems
Spicebush (Lindera benzoin)	8.4	2.6
Multiflora rosa (Rosa multiflora)	4.6	4.3
Allegheny blackberry (Rubus allegheniensis)	0.9	0.6
Southern arrowwod (Viburnum dentatum)	0.6	1.0
Blackhaw (Viburnum prunifolium)	0.3	0.2
Autumn olive (Elaeagnus umbellata)	0.1	0.1
Morrow's honeysuckle (Lonicera morrowii)	0.1	0.1

Table 6. Average plot and quadrat species richness in Fort Necessity National Battlefield (FONE) and Friendship Hill National Historic Site (FRHI).

	FONE		FRHI
Diversity measure	Oak/Tuliptree Forest (n=6)	Successional Forest (n=4)	(n=10)
Plot richness	48	38	36
Quadrat richness	13.2	9.1	11.2

Table 7. Average values for percent of total quadrat cover and species richness of nonnative and native species calculated from monitoring plots in Fort Necessity National Battlefield (FONE) and Friendship Hill National Historic Site (FRHI).

Diversity measure	Nonnative species	Native species
FONE Oak/Tuliptree Forest (n=6)		
Percent of total cover	2.4%	94.4%
Percent of species richness	2.8%	89.5%
FONE Successional Forest (n=4)		
Percent of total cover	34.7%	60.1%
Percent of species richness	16.9%	71.3%
FRHI (n=10)		
Percent of total cover	31.4%	65.5%
Percent of species richness	17.9%	73.7%

Table 8. Number of monitoring plots in which invasive exotic plant species were observed in Fort Necessity National Battlefield (FONE) and Friendship Hill National Historic Site (FRHI) between 2007–2009.

Common name	Scientific name	Number of plots in FONE (n=15)	Number of plots in FRHI (n=15)
multiflora rose	*Rosa multiflora*	9	12
Japanese barberry	*Berberis thunbergii*	8	2
Japanese stiltgrass	*Microstegium vimineum*		8
Japanese honeysuckle	*Lonicera japonica*		8
Oriental ladysthumb	*Polygonum caespitosum*	4	7
Morrow's honeysuckle	*Lonicera morrowii*	7	3
ground ivy	*Glechoma hederacea*	1	6
sweet vernalgrass	*Anthoxanthum odoratum*	3	1
tree of heaven	*Ailanthus altissima*		5
autumn olive	*Elaeagnus umbellata*		2
burningbush	*Euonymus alatus*	1	
bull thistle	*Cirsium vulgare*	1	
garlic mustard	*Alliaria petiolata*		1

Deer Browse Indicators

Data on numerous herbaceous plant species that are considered sensitive to deer browse are being collected. In general, these species are less common than in other ERMN parks. No indicator species were found in more than 27% of the plots in FRHI, with mayapple (*Podophyllum peltatum*) being the most common species. In FONE, both Indian cucumber (*Medeola virginiana*) and perfoliate bellwort (*Uvularia perfoliata*) were found in one-third of the park's plots. The number of reproducing, non-reproducing, browsed, and non-browsed plants in each quadrat is collected, along with the height of the three tallest plants in each quadrat. We will be looking for changes in these variables through time to gauge the survival and persistence of these species.

Habitat Diversity

Biotic homogenization is the process by which regional biodiversity declines through time due to the addition of widespread exotic species as well as the loss of native species (Olden & Rooney 2006). Homogenization occurs when the variety of different vegetation types within a park become more similar to each other, shifting from specialized unique vegetation communities towards a more generic homogeneous species composition throughout. Biotic homogenization can be caused by many factors, including land use change, climate change, soil fertility, deer browse, and invasive exotic animal and plant species.

Jaccard's similarity index can be used to evaluate biotic homogenization by comparing the similarity between the species composition of any two plots. The average Jaccard's index for the park includes all possible between-plot comparisons and provides a measure of the diversity of habitats in the park. The average Jaccard's index for FONE monitoring plots is 0.175. Within FRHI, the average Jaccard's index is 0.164.

Tracking the change in Jaccard's index through time will provide information on the extent and magnitude of biotic homogenization within the park. Through time, an increase in the average Jaccard's index would indicate that the park's vegetation types are becoming less diverse.

Lists of all of the vascular plant taxa observed in monitoring plots between 2007 and 2009 are provided in Appendix A for FONE and Appendix B for FRHI.

Invasive Exotic Plant Species

Thirteen invasive exotic plant species were observed in the monitoring plots (Table 8) between 2007 and 2009. Only 27% of the plots were free of invasive plant species in FONE, while 60% of the plots contained two or more invasive plant species. In FRHI, 20% of the plots were free of invasive plant species, while 67% of the plots contained two or more invasive plant species.

The most commonly observed invasive exotic plant species in both parks was multiflora rose (*Rosa multiflora*), which occurred in 80% of the FHRI plots and 60% of the FONE plots. Japanese barberry (*Berberis thunbergii*), Oriental ladysthumb (*Polygonum caespitosum*), Morrow's honeysuckle (*Lonicera morrowii*), and ground ivy (*Glechoma hederacea*) were common in both parks. In FRHI, Japanese stiltgrass (*Microstegium vimineum*) and Japanese honeysuckle (*Lonicera japonica*) were also common (observed in 53% of plots).

Early Detection of Exotic Invasive Plants and Animals

No species from the early detection terrestrial plant and forest pest/pathogen watch lists were observed in FONE between 2007 and 2009.

In 2008, privet (*Ligustrum* sp.) was detected at FRHI in a field to the west of New Geneva Road (PA 166), off Pekar Road. Privet covered 50–100 m^2 in the field, suggesting that the species has been established in the field for several years. The location of the privet was reported to park natural resource managers in accordance with the ERMN Invasive Species Early Detection and Rapid Response protocol (Keefer et al. 2009).

Discussion

This report summarized the vegetation monitoring data collected between 2007 and 2009 in Fort Necessity National Battlefield (FONE) and Friendship Hill National Historic Park (FHRI) and presented the condition of the parks' vegetation as compared to expected ranges of variability for eastern forest systems. In general, forests in both parks are typical of other second-growth forests in the Appalachian Mountains; however, the results from the monitoring data underscore two important points for park managers: 1) invasive exotic plant species are a pervasive and spreading threat to the parks' resources; and 2) factors contributing to poor tree regeneration, particularly of oaks, need to be investigated further in order to evaluate potential management actions.

That invasive exotic plant species are a serious and growing threat to park resources is not a novel assertion. The monitoring data concur with previous research in the parks documenting that invasive exotic species are pervasive, especially in young or successional forests and in successional areas that were formerly agricultural or recently disturbed (Zimmerman and Yoder 2006). These findings underscore the vital importance of the many ongoing projects in FONE and FRHI directed by park managers, the Southern Laurel Highlands Plant Management Partnership's Project Weed Whack, and external researchers that are addressing invasive exotic plants. When possible, additional resources should be strategically allocated to managing invasive exotic species through the following actions:

a) Remove invasive exotic plants from areas of the parks in which invasive species are less abundant (e.g. oak- and tuliptree-dominated forests of FONE's Main Unit).
b) Detect and eliminate (when possible) new populations of invasive exotic species novel to the parks (implementation of the Early Detection and Rapid Response protocol).
c) Work with partners to acquire and release approved biological controls for invasive exotic species that are widespread and abundant in the parks.

Poor tree regeneration, especially in oak species (*Quercus* spp.), has been documented widely in Pennsylvania and surrounding areas. This regeneration failure could be attributed to one or more of the following factors: dense shade from canopy or sub-canopy trees; competition from shrubs, ferns, or grasses; and/or altered disturbance regimes, including fire suppression; browse pressure from white-tailed deer; and/or soil infertility. Most forest stands in the parks are closed-canopy with few canopy gaps that are critical for oak regeneration. Without the periodic surface fires and occasional canopy gaps that perpetuated oak forests in previous centuries (Brose et al 2008), oak seedlings are at a competitive disadvantage to other tree species (Abrams 1998). Stands with ideal conditions for oak regeneration contain less than 70% stocking of the canopy and less than 70% cover in the groundstory of competing vegetation such as shrubs, ferns, and grasses (Brose et al 2008). Many of the young and middle-aged forest stands in FRHI and FONE may not meet these requirements for regeneration simply due to their age.

In addition, changes in land use and land management over previous decades have led to expanded native white-tailed deer populations (Latham et al. 2005). Selective browsing by deer leads to altered species composition towards dominance of non-preferred and browse-resilient tree species, such as maples (*Acer* spp.) and birches (*Betula* spp.), along with overall reduced survival of tree seedlings and saplings, especially of browse-preferred species such as oaks

(Russell et al. 2001, Horsley et al. 2003, Latham et al. 2005). Another confounding factor for some tree species may be soil infertility. Acid deposition can have significant effects on soils, including depletion of base cations such as calcium and magnesium, and the mobilization of aluminum and manganese (Driscoll et al. 2001). These changes in soil chemistry have been linked to decreases in sugar maple (*Acer saccharum*) seedlings and increases in hay-scented fern (*Dennstaedtia punctilobula*) cover, which generally inhibits seedling growth (Sharpe and Halofsky 2004).

As more data on both vegetation and soil are collected from the monitoring plots we will investigate correlations between the factors discussed above and tree regeneration in FONE and FRHI. We hope to be able to provide guidance on potential management actions (including "let the forest grow old") pertaining to forest regeneration.

Literature Cited

Abrams, M. 1998. The red maple paradox. BioScience 48(5):355–364.

Brose, P. H., K. W. Gottschalk, S. B. Horsley, P. D. Knopp, J. N. Kochenderfer, B. J. McGuinness, G. W. Miller, T. E. Ristau, S. H. Stoleson, and S. L. Stout. 2008. Prescribing regeneration treatments for mixed-oak forests in the Mid-Atlantic region. Gen. Tech. Rep. NRS-33. Newtown Square, PA: U.S. Department of Agriculture, Forest Service, Northern Research Station. 100 pp.

Carey, A. B. 1983. Cavities in trees in hardwood forests. Pp 167–184. *In* Snag habitat management: Proc. Symp., J. W. Davis, G. A. Goodwin, and R. A. Ockenfels, Technical Coordinators. USDA Forest Service General Technical Report. RM-99. 226 pp.

Comiskey, J. A., J. P. Schmit, and G. Tierney. 2009. Mid-Atlantic Network forest vegetation monitoring protocol. Natural Resource Report NPS/MIDN/NRR—2009/119. National Park Service, Fort Collins, CO.

Curtis, R. O., and D. D. Marshall. 2000. Why quadratic mean diameter? Western Journal of Applied Forestry. 15(3):137–139.

Driscoll, C. T., G. B. Lawrence, A. J. Bulger, T. J. Butler, C. S. Cronan, C. Eagar, K. F. Lambert, G. E. Likens, J. L. Stoddard, and K. C. Weathers. 2001. Acidic deposition in the northeastern United States: sources and inputs, ecosystem effects, and management strategies. BioScience 51(3):180–198.

Fancy, S. G., J. E. Gross, and S. L. Carter. 2009. Monitoring the condition of natural resources in U.S. national parks. Environmental Monitoring and Assessment 151:161–174.

Frelich, L. E., and C. G. Lorimer. 1991. Natural disturbance regimes in hemlock-hardwood forests of the upper Great Lakes region. Ecological Monographs. 61:145–164

Goodburn, J. M., and C.G. Lorimer. 1998. Cavity trees and coarse woody debris in old-growth and managed northern hardwood forests in Wisconsin and Michigan. Canadian Journal of Forest Research. 28:427–438.

Keefer, J. S., M. R. Marshall, and B. R. Mitchell. 2009. Early detection of invasive species—surveillance and rapid response for the Eastern Rivers and Mountains and Northeast Temperate networks. Natural Resource Report NPS/ERMN/NRR–2009/XXX. National Park Service, Fort Collins, CO.

Harmon, M. E., J. F. Franklin, F. J. Swanson, P. Sollins, S. V. Gregory, J. D. Lattin, N. H. Anderson, S. P. Cline, N. G. Aumen, J. R. Sedell, S. W. Liekaemper, D. Cromack, Jr., and K. W. Cumins. 1983. Ecology of coarse woody debris in temperate ecosystems. Advances in Ecological Research. 15:133–302.

Horsely, S. B., S. L. Stout, and D. S. DeCalesta. 2003. White-tailed deer impact on the vegetation dynamics of a northern hardwood forest. Ecological Applications 13(1):98–118.

Latham, R. E., J. Beyea, M. Benner, C. A. Dunn, M. A. Fajvan, R. R. Freed, M. Grund, S. B. Horsley, A. F. Rhoads, and B. P. Shissler. 2005. Managing white-tailed deer in forest habitat from an ecosystem perspective: Pennsylvania case study. Report by the Deer Management Forum for Audubon Pennsylvania and Pennsylvania Habitat Alliance, Harrisburg. 340 pp.

Marshall, M. R., and N. B. Piekielek. 2007. Eastern Rivers and Mountains Network Ecological Monitoring Plan. Natural Resource Report NPS/ERMN/NRR—2007/017. National Park Service, Fort Collins, CO.

McComb, W. C., and R. N. Muller. 1983. Snag densities in old-growth and second-growth Appalachian forests. The Journal of Wildlife Management. 47(2):376–382.

McDonald, T. L. 2004. GRTS for the average Joe: A GRTS sampler for Windows. http://www.west-inc.com/biometrics_reports.php.

McWilliams, W. H.; S. L. King, and C. T. Scott. 2001. Assessing regeneration adequacy in Pennsylvania's forests: a pilot study. *In* Reams, G. L., R. E. McRoberts, and P. C. Van Deusen, eds. Proceedings, 2d annual Forest Inventory and Analysis symposium. 2000 October 17–18. Salt Lake City, UT. Gen. Tech. Rep. SRS-47. Asheville, NC: U.S. Department of Agriculture, Forest Service, Southern Research Station. Pp. 119–122.

McWilliams, W. H., T. W. Bowersox, P. H. Brose, D. A. Devlin, J. C. Finley, K. W. Gottschalk, S. Horsley, S. L. King, B. M. LaPoint, T. W. Lister, L. H. McCormick, G. W. Miller, C. T. Scott, H. Steele, K. C. Steiner, S. L. Stout, J. A. Westfall1, and R. L. White. 2005. Measuring tree seedlings and associated understory vegetation in Pennsylvania's forests. *In* R. E. McRoberts, G. A. Reams, P. C. Van Deusen, W. H. McWilliams, and C. J. Cieszewski, eds. 2005. Proceedings of the fourth annual Forest Inventory and Analysis symposium 2002 November 19–21. New Orleans, LA. Gen. Tech. Rep. NC-252. St. Paul, MN: U.S. Department of Agriculture, Forest Service, North Central Research Station. 257 pp.

Muller, R. N., and Y. Liu. 1991. Coarse woody debris in an old-growth deciduous forest on the Cumberland Plateau, southeastern Kentucky. Canadian Journal of Forest Research. 21:1567–1572.

Olden, J. D., and T. P. Rooney. 2006. On defining and quantifying biotic homogenization. Global Ecology and Biogeography 15(2):113–120.

Perles, S., J. Finley, and M. Marshall. 2009. Vegetation monitoring protocol for the Eastern Rivers and Mountains Network, version 1. Natural Resource Report NPS/ERMN/NRR—2009/DRAFT. National Park Service, Fort Collins, CO.

Rentch, J. S. 2006. Structure and functioning of terrestrial ecosystems in the Eastern Rivers and Mountains Network: Conceptual models and vital signs monitoring. Natural Resources Report NPS/NER/NRR—2006/007. National Park Service, Philadelphia, PA.

Rosenberg, D. K., J. D. Fraser, and D. F. Stauffer. 1988. Use and characteristics of snags in young and old forest stands in southwest Virginia. Forest Science. 34(1):224–228.

Runkle, J. R. 1998. Changes in Southern Appalachian canopy tree gaps sampled thrice. Ecology 79(5):1768–1780.

Runkle, J. R. 2000. Canopy tree turnover in old-growth mesic forests in eastern North America. Ecology 81(2):554–567.

Russell, F. L, D. B. Zippin, and N. L. Fowler. 2001. Effects of white-tailed deer (*Odocoileus virginianus)* on plants, plant populations, and communities: a review. American Midland Naturalist 146(1):1–26.

Sanders, S., S. E. Johnson, and D. M. Waller. 2006. General vegetation monitoring protocol for the Great Lakes Network, Version 1.0. National Park Service, Great Lakes Network, Ashland, WI.

Schmit, J. P., D. C. Chojnacky, and M. Milton. 2006. Forest Monitoring Protocol, Version 1.0. National Park Service, National Capital Region Network, Washington, DC.

Sharpe, W. E., and J. E. Halofsky. 2004. Hay-scented fern (*Dennstaedtia punctilobula*) and sugar maple (*Acer saccharum*) seedling occurrence with varying soil acidity in Pennsylvania. Proceedings of the 14th Central Hardwood Forest Conference: 2004 March 16–19; Wooster, OH. Gen. Tech. Rep. NE-316. U.S. Department of Agriculture, Forest Service, Northeastern Research Station. Pp. 265–270.

Stevens, D. L., and A. N. Olsen. 2004. Spatially balanced sampling of natural resources. Journal of American Statistical Association 99(465):262–278.

Tierney, G., and D. Faber-Langendoen. 2007. NPS Northeast Temperate Network Long-term Forest Monitoring Protocol. Natural Resources Report NPS/NETN/NRR—XXXX/XXX. National Park Service. Fort Collins, CO.

Tierney, G. L., D. Faber-Langendoen, B. R. Mitchell, W. G. Shriver, and J. P. Gibbs. 2009. Monitoring and evaluating the ecological integrity of forest ecosystems. Frontiers in Ecology and the Environment.7, doi.10.1890/070176

Tritton, L. M., and T. G. Siccama. 1990. What proportion of standing trees in forests of the Northeast are dead? Bulletin of the Torrey Botanical Club 117:163–166.

United States Department of Agriculture (USDA), Natural Resource Conservation Service (NRCS). 2007. The PLANTS Database (http://plants.usda.gov). National Plant Data Center, Baton Rouge, LA 70874-4490 USA.

United States Forest Service (USFS). 2007. Forest Inventory and Analysis National Core Field Guide. Version 4.0. United States Forest Service. 224 pp.

Van Wagner, C. E. 1964. The line-intersect method in forest fuel sampling. Forest Science 28:267–276.

Zimmerman, E., and J. Yoder. 2006. Distribution and abundance of nonnative plant species at Fort Necessity National Battlefield and Friendship Hill National Historic Site. Natural Resource Technical Report NPS/NER/NRTR—2006/053. National Park Service, Philadelphia, PA.

Appendix A. Plants observed in Fort Necessity National Battlefield during vegetation monitoring plot sampling, 2007–2009.

Nomenclature follows the Master Plant List in the Vegetation and Soil Monitoring Database (Perles et al 2009), which is based on the USDA PLANTS Database (USDA, NRCS 2007).

Family	Latin_name	Common
Aceraceae	Acer rubrum	red maple
	Acer saccharum	sugar maple
	Acer sp.	maple
Alismataceae	Sagittaria latifolia	broadleaf arrowhead
Anacardiaceae	Toxicodendron radicans	eastern poison ivy
Apiaceae	Hydrocotyle americana	American marshpennywort
	Osmorhiza claytonii	Clayton's sweetroot
	Sanicula canadensis	Canadian blacksnakeroot
	Sanicula sp.	sanicle
Apocynaceae	Apocynum cannabinum	Indianhemp
Aquifoliaceae	Ilex verticillata	common winterberry
Araceae	Arisaema triphyllum	Jack in the pulpit
	Symplocarpus foetidus	skunk cabbage
Araliaceae	Aralia nudicaulis	wild sarsaparilla
	Aralia spinosa	devil's walkingstick
Aristolochiaceae	Aristolochia serpentaria	Virginia snakeroot
Asteraceae	Achillea millefolium	common yarrow
	Ageratina altissima	white snakeroot
	Arctium minus	lesser burdock
	Bidens sp.	beggarticks
	Cirsium vulgare	bull thistle
	Erechtites hieraciifolia	American burnweed
	Eurybia divaricata	white wood aster
	Euthamia graminifolia	flat-top goldentop
	Hieracium sp.	hawkweed
	Hieracium venosum	rattlesnakeweed
	Hypochaeris radicata	hairy catsear
	Leucanthemum vulgare	oxeye daisy
	Packera aurea	golden ragwort
	Prenanthes sp.	rattlesnakeroot
	Solidago caesia	wreath goldenrod
	Solidago gigantea	giant goldenrod
	Solidago juncea	early goldenrod
	Solidago rugosa	wrinkleleaf goldenrod
	Solidago sp.	goldenrod
	Symphyotrichum prenanthoides	crookedstem aster
	Symphyotrichum sp.	aster
	Vernonia noveboracensis	New York ironweed
Balsaminaceae	Impatiens capensis	jewelweed
	Impatiens sp.	touch-me-not
Berberidaceae	Berberis thunbergii	Japanese barberry
	Caulophyllum thalictroides	blue cohosh
	Podophyllum peltatum	mayapple
Betulaceae	Betula lenta	sweet birch
	Betula sp.	birch
	Carpinus caroliniana	American hornbeam

Family	Latin_name	Common
Betulaceae (cont)	*Ostrya virginiana*	hophornbeam
Boraginaceae	*Cynoglossum officinale*	gypsyflower
	Cynoglossum virginianum	wild comfrey
Caprifoliaceae	*Lonicera morrowii*	Morrow's honeysuckle
	Sambucus nigra ssp. *canadensis*	common elderberry
	Viburnum acerifolium	mapleleaf viburnum
	Viburnum dentatum	southern arrowwood
	Viburnum lentago	nannyberry
Caryophyllaceae	*Stellaria pubera*	star chickweed
Celastraceae	*Euonymus alatus*	burningbush
	Euonymus americanus	bursting-heart
Clusiaceae	*Hypericum perforatum*	common St. Johnswort
	Hypericum punctatum	spotted St. Johnswort
Convolvulaceae	*Calystegia sepium*	hedge false bindweed
Cornaceae	*Cornus alternifolia*	alternateleaf dogwood
	Cornus florida	flowering dogwood
	Cornus sp.	dogwood
	Nyssa sylvatica	blackgum
Crassulaceae	*Sedum ternatum*	woodland stonecrop
Cyperaceae	*Carex appalachica*	Appalachian sedge
	Carex blanda	eastern woodland sedge
	Carex debilis	white edge sedge
	Carex digitalis	slender woodland sedge
	Carex gracilescens	slender looseflower sedge
	Carex gracillima	graceful sedge
	Carex gynandra	nodding sedge
	Carex hirsutella	fuzzy wuzzy sedge
	Carex intumescens	greater bladder sedge
	Carex laxiculmis	spreading sedge
	Carex laxiculmis var. *laxiculmis*	spreading sedge
	Carex laxiflora	broad looseflower sedge
	Carex lurida	shallow sedge
	Carex plantaginea	plantainleaf sedge
	Carex radiata	eastern star sedge
	Carex rosea	rosy sedge
	Carex sp.	sedge
	Carex swanii	Swan's sedge
	Carex vesicaria	blister sedge
	Scirpus polyphyllus	leafy bulrush
Dennstaedtiaceae	*Dennstaedtia punctilobula*	eastern hayscented fern
Dioscoreaceae	*Dioscorea quaternata*	fourleaf yam
	Dioscorea villosa	wild yam
Dryopteridaceae	*Athyrium filix-femina*	common ladyfern
	Deparia acrostichoides	silver false spleenwort
	Dryopteris carthusiana	spinulose woodfern
	Dryopteris intermedia	intermediate woodfern
	Dryopteris marginalis	marginal woodfern
	Onoclea sensibilis	sensitive fern
	Polystichum acrostichoides	Christmas fern
Ericaceae	*Gaultheria procumbens*	eastern teaberry
	Gaylussacia baccata	black huckleberry
	Rhododendron sp.	rhododendron

Family	Latin_name	Common
Ericaceae (cont)	Vaccinium angustifolium	lowbush blueberry
	Vaccinium corymbosum	highbush blueberry
	Vaccinium pallidum	Blue Ridge blueberry
	Vaccinium sp.	blueberry
	Vaccinium stamineum	deerberry
Fabaceae	Amphicarpaea bracteata	American hogpeanut
	Desmodium sp.	ticktrefoil
	Lespedeza sp.	lespedeza
	Robinia pseudoacacia	black locust
	Trifolium pratense	red clover
	Trifolium sp.	clover
Fagaceae	Castanea dentata	American chestnut
	Fagus grandifolia	American beech
	Quercus alba	white oak
	Quercus prinus	chestnut oak
	Quercus rubra	northern red oak
	Quercus velutina	black oak
Geraniaceae	Geranium maculatum	spotted geranium
Grossulariaceae	Ribes sp.	currant
Hamamelidaceae	Hamamelis virginiana	American witchhazel
Iridaceae	Iris sp.	iris
	Sisyrinchium sp.	blue-eyed grass
Juglandaceae	Carya alba	mockernut hickory
	Carya glabra	pignut hickory
	Carya ovata	shagbark hickory
	Carya sp.	hickory
Juncaceae	Juncus effusus	common rush
	Juncus sp.	rush
	Juncus tenuis	poverty rush
	Luzula multiflora	common woodrush
Lamiaceae	Clinopodium vulgare	wild basil
	Glechoma hederacea	ground ivy
	Lycopus sp.	waterhorehound
	Lycopus uniflorus	northern bugleweed
	Prunella vulgaris	common selfheal
	Scutellaria sp.	skullcap
Lauraceae	Lindera benzoin	northern spicebush
	Sassafras albidum	sassafras
Liliaceae	Clintonia umbellulata	white clintonia
	Lilium sp.	lily
	Maianthemum racemosum	feathery false lily of the valley
	Medeola virginiana	Indian cucumber
	Polygonatum biflorum	smooth Solomon's seal
	Polygonatum pubescens	hairy Solomon's seal
	Prosartes lanuginosa	yellow fairybells
	Uvularia perfoliata	perfoliate bellwort
	Uvularia sessilifolia	sessileleaf bellwort
	Veratrum viride	green false hellebore
Lycopodiaceae	Lycopodium digitatum	fan clubmoss
Magnoliaceae	Liriodendron tulipifera	tuliptree
	Magnolia acuminata	cucumber-tree
Monotropaceae	Monotropa uniflora	Indianpipe

Family	Latin_name	Common
Oleaceae	*Fraxinus americana*	white ash
	Fraxinus nigra	black ash
Onagraceae	*Circaea lutetiana*	broadleaf enchanter's nightshade
Ophioglossaceae	*Botrychium dissectum*	cutleaf grapefern
	Botrychium virginianum	rattlesnake fern
Orchidaceae	*Cypripedium* sp.	lady's slipper
	Goodyera pubescens	downy rattlesnake plantain
Orobanchaceae	*Conopholis americana*	American cancer-root
Osmundaceae	*Osmunda cinnamomea*	cinnamon fern
	Osmunda claytoniana	interrupted fern
Oxalidaceae	*Oxalis stricta*	common yellow oxalis
Phytolaccaceae	*Phytolacca americana*	American pokeweed
Pinaceae	*Picea abies*	Norway spruce
	Picea glauca	white spruce
	Pinus strobus	eastern white pine
	Pinus sylvestris	Scots pine
Poaceae	*Agrostis gigantea*	redtop
	Agrostis perennans	upland bentgrass
	Anthoxanthum odoratum	sweet vernalgrass
	Arrhenatherum elatius var. *elatius*	tall oatgrass
	Brachyelytrum erectum	bearded shorthusk
	Cinna arundinacea	sweet woodreed
	Dactylis glomerata	orchardgrass
	Danthonia compressa	flattened oatgrass
	Danthonia spicata	poverty oatgrass
	Dichanthelium acuminatum	tapered rosette grass
	Dichanthelium boscii	Bosc's panicgrass
	Dichanthelium clandestinum	deertongue
	Dichanthelium dichotomum	cypress panicgrass
	Dichanthelium latifolium	broadleaf rosette grass
	Dichanthelium sp.	rosette grass
	Elymus repens	quackgrass
	Glyceria canadensis	rattlesnake mannagrass
	Glyceria striata	fowl mannagrass
	Holcus lanatus	common velvetgrass
	Leersia oryzoides	rice cutgrass
	Leersia virginica	whitegrass
	Panicum sp.	panicgrass
	Phleum pratense	timothy
	Poa alsodes	grove bluegrass
	Poa sp.	bluegrass
Polygalaceae	*Polygala paucifolia*	gaywings
Polygonaceae	*Polygonum caespitosum*	Oriental ladysthumb
	Polygonum sagittatum	arrowleaf tearthumb
	Polygonum scandens	climbing false buckwheat
	Polygonum virginianum	jumpseed
	Rumex acetosella	common sheep sorrel
	Rumex obtusifolius	bitter dock
Primulaceae	*Lysimachia quadrifolia*	whorled yellow loosestrife
Pyrolaceae	*Pyrola* sp.	wintergreen
Ranunculaceae	*Actaea racemosa*	black baneberry
	Clematis virginiana	devil's darning needles

Family	Latin_name	Common
Ranunculaceae (cont)	*Ranunculus abortivus*	littleleaf buttercup
	Ranunculus recurvatus	blisterwort
	Thalictrum pubescens	king of the meadow
	Thalictrum thalictroides	rue anemone
Rosaceae	*Agrimonia* sp.	agrimony
	Amelanchier arborea	common serviceberry
	Amelanchier sp.	serviceberry
	Crataegus sp.	hawthorn
	Fragaria virginiana	Virginia strawberry
	Geum sp.	avens
	Malus sp.	apple
	Physocarpus opulifolius	common ninebark
	Potentilla simplex	common cinquefoil
	Prunus avium	sweet cherry
	Prunus serotina	black cherry
	Prunus sp.	plum
	Rosa multiflora	multiflora rose
	Rubus allegheniensis	Allegheny blackberry
	Rubus hispidus	bristly dewberry
	Rubus sp.	blackberry
	Spiraea alba	white meadowsweet
Rubiaceae	*Galium asprellum*	rough bedstraw
	Galium circaezans	licorice bedstraw
	Galium lanceolatum	lanceleaf wild licorice
	Galium triflorum	fragrant bedstraw
	Mitchella repens	partridgeberry
Salicaceae	*Populus grandidentata*	bigtooth aspen
Saxifragaceae	*Heuchera* sp.	alumroot
Scrophulariaceae	*Gratiola neglecta*	clammy hedgehyssop
	Veronica officinalis	common gypsyweed
Smilacaceae	*Smilax glauca*	cat greenbrier
	Smilax herbacea	smooth carrionflower
	Smilax rotundifolia	roundleaf greenbrier
	Smilax sp.	greenbrier
	Smilax tamnoides	bristly greenbrier
Solanaceae	*Solanum carolinense*	Carolina horsenettle
Thelypteridaceae	*Thelypteris noveboracensis*	New York fern
Ulmaceae	*Ulmus* sp.	elm
Urticaceae	*Pilea pumila*	Canadian clearweed
Violaceae	*Viola* ×*palmata*	early blue violet
	Viola hastata	halberdleaf yellow violet
	Viola pubescens	downy yellow violet
	Viola rotundifolia	roundleaf yellow violet
	Viola sororia	common blue violet
	Viola sp.	violet
	Viola striata	striped cream violet
Vitaceae	*Parthenocissus quinquefolia*	Virginia creeper
	Vitis aestivalis	summer grape
	Vitis sp.	grape

Appendix B. Plants observed in Friendship Hill National Historic Site during vegetation monitoring plot sampling, 2007–2009.

Nomenclature follows the Master Plant List in the Vegetation and Soil Monitoring Database (Perles et al 2009), which is based on the USDA PLANTS Database (USDA, NRCS 2007).

Family	Latin name	Common
Aceraceae	*Acer negundo*	boxelder
	Acer rubrum	red maple
	Acer saccharinum	silver maple
	Acer saccharum	sugar maple
	Acer sp.	maple
Alismataceae	*Sagittaria* sp.	arrowhead
Anacardiaceae	*Toxicodendron radicans*	eastern poison ivy
Annonaceae	*Asimina triloba*	pawpaw
Apiaceae	*Cryptotaenia canadensis*	Canadian honewort
	Osmorhiza claytonii	Clayton's sweetroot
	Pastinaca sativa	wild parsnip
	Sanicula canadensis	Canadian blacksnakeroot
	Sanicula sp.	sanicle
Apocynaceae	*Apocynum* sp.	dogbane
Aquifoliaceae	*Ilex verticillata*	common winterberry
Araceae	*Arisaema triphyllum*	Jack in the pulpit
Araliaceae	*Panax quinquefolius*	American ginseng
Aspleniaceae	*Asplenium platyneuron*	ebony spleenwort
Asteraceae	*Ageratina altissima*	white snakeroot
	Ambrosia artemisiifolia	annual ragweed
	Aster sp.	aster
	Erechtites hieraciifolia	American burnweed
	Erigeron annuus	eastern daisy fleabane
	Erigeron philadelphicus	Philadelphia fleabane
	Erigeron sp.	fleabane
	Eupatoriadelphus maculatus var. *maculatus*	spotted trumpetweed
	Eurybia divaricata	white wood aster
	Euthamia graminifolia	flat-top goldentop
	Lactuca sp.	lettuce
	Packera aurea	golden ragwort
	Prenanthes sp.	rattlesnakeroot
	Solidago caesia	wreath goldenrod
	Solidago gigantea	giant goldenrod
	Solidago juncea	early goldenrod
	Solidago rugosa	wrinkleleaf goldenrod
	Solidago sp.	goldenrod
	Symphyotrichum lateriflorum	calico aster
	Symphyotrichum prenanthoides	crookedstem aster
	Taraxacum officinale	common dandelion
	Verbesina alternifolia	wingstem
	Verbesina occidentalis	yellow crownbeard
	Vernonia noveboracensis	New York ironweed
Balsaminaceae	*Impatiens capensis*	jewelweed
	Impatiens sp.	touch-me-not
Berberidaceae	*Berberis thunbergii*	Japanese barberry

Family	Latin_name	Common
Berberidaceae (cont)	*Caulophyllum thalictroides*	blue cohosh
	Podophyllum peltatum	mayapple
Betulaceae	*Betula lenta*	sweet birch
	Betula sp.	birch
	Ostrya virginiana	hophornbeam
Bignoniaceae	*Catalpa speciosa*	northern catalpa
Boraginaceae	*Hackelia virginiana*	beggarslice
Brassicaceae	*Alliaria petiolata*	garlic mustard
	Cardamine hirsuta	hairy bittercress
Campanulaceae	*Lobelia* sp.	lobelia
Caprifoliaceae	*Lonicera japonica*	Japanese honeysuckle
	Lonicera morrowii	Morrow's honeysuckle
	Viburnum acerifolium	mapleleaf viburnum
	Viburnum dentatum	southern arrowwood
	Viburnum prunifolium	blackhaw
Caryophyllaceae	*Cerastium fontanum*	common mouse-ear chickweed
	Stellaria pubera	star chickweed
Convolvulaceae	*Calystegia sepium*	hedge false bindweed
	Convolvulus arvensis	field bindweed
Cornaceae	*Cornus alternifolia*	alternateleaf dogwood
	Cornus florida	flowering dogwood
	Nyssa sylvatica	blackgum
Crassulaceae	*Sedum ternatum*	woodland stonecrop
Cuscutaceae	*Cuscuta gronovii*	scaldweed
Cyperaceae	*Carex albursina*	white bear sedge
	Carex annectens	yellowfruit sedge
	Carex bushii	Bush's sedge
	Carex crinita var. *crinita*	fringed sedge
	Carex digitalis	slender woodland sedge
	Carex hirsutella	fuzzy wuzzy sedge
	Carex laxiculmis	spreading sedge
	Carex laxiflora	broad looseflower sedge
	Carex leptonervia	nerveless woodland sedge
	Carex radiata	eastern star sedge
	Carex rosea	rosy sedge
	Carex sp.	sedge
	Carex swanii	Swan's sedge
	Carex vulpinoidea	fox sedge
	Carex willdenowii	Willdenow's sedge
	Scirpus polyphyllus	leafy bulrush
Dennstaedtiaceae	*Dennstaedtia punctilobula*	eastern hayscented fern
Dioscoreaceae	*Dioscorea villosa*	wild yam
Dryopteridaceae	*Athyrium filix-femina*	common ladyfern
	Deparia acrostichoides	silver false spleenwort
	Dryopteris carthusiana	spinulose woodfern
	Dryopteris marginalis	marginal woodfern
	Matteuccia struthiopteris	ostrich fern
	Onoclea sensibilis	sensitive fern
	Polystichum acrostichoides	Christmas fern
Elaeagnaceae	*Elaeagnus umbellata*	autumn olive
Fabaceae	*Amphicarpaea bracteata*	American hogpeanut
	Desmodium sp.	ticktrefoil

Family	Latin_name	Common
Fabaceae (cont)	Gleditsia triacanthos	honeylocust
	Robinia pseudoacacia	black locust
Fagaceae	Fagus grandifolia	American beech
	Quercus alba	white oak
	Quercus palustris	pin oak
	Quercus rubra	northern red oak
	Quercus sp.	oak
	Quercus velutina	black oak
Geraniaceae	Geranium maculatum	spotted geranium
Hydrophyllaceae	Hydrophyllum canadense	bluntleaf waterleaf
	Hydrophyllum virginianum	eastern waterleaf
Iridaceae	Sisyrinchium angustifolium	narrowleaf blue-eyed grass
Juglandaceae	Carya alba	mockernut hickory
	Carya cordiformis	bitternut hickory
	Carya sp.	hickory
	Juglans nigra	black walnut
Juncaceae	Juncus effusus	common rush
	Juncus tenuis	poverty rush
Lamiaceae	Clinopodium vulgare	wild basil
	Glechoma hederacea	ground ivy
	Mentha arvensis	wild mint
	Prunella vulgaris	common selfheal
	Pycnanthemum incanum	hoary mountainmint
	Pycnanthemum tenuifolium	narrowleaf mountainmint
	Scutellaria sp.	skullcap
	Teucrium canadense	Canada germander
Lauraceae	Lindera benzoin	northern spicebush
	Sassafras albidum	sassafras
Liliaceae	Maianthemum racemosum	feathery false lily of the valley
	Medeola virginiana	Indian cucumber
	Polygonatum biflorum	smooth Solomon's seal
	Polygonatum pubescens	hairy Solomon's seal
Magnoliaceae	Liriodendron tulipifera	tuliptree
Oleaceae	Forsythia sp.	forsythia
	Fraxinus americana	white ash
	Fraxinus sp.	ash
	Ligustrum sp.	privet
Onagraceae	Circaea lutetiana	broadleaf enchanter's nightshade
	Epilobium sp.	willowherb
Ophioglossaceae	Botrychium dissectum	cutleaf grapefern
	Botrychium virginianum	rattlesnake fern
	Ophioglossum pusillum	northern adderstongue
	Ophioglossum sp.	adderstongue
Orchidaceae	Galearis spectabilis	showy orchid
	Goodyera pubescens	downy rattlesnake plantain
Orobanchaceae	Conopholis americana	American cancer-root
Oxalidaceae	Oxalis stricta	common yellow oxalis
Phytolaccaceae	Phytolacca americana	American pokeweed
Pinaceae	Larix sp.	larch
	Picea abies	Norway spruce
	Pinus sp.	pine
	Pinus strobus	eastern white pine

Family	Latin_name	Common
Plantaginaceae	*Plantago virginica*	Virginia plantain
Platanaceae	*Platanus occidentalis*	American sycamore
Poaceae	*Agrostis hyemalis*	winter bentgrass
	Agrostis sp.	bentgrass
	Anthoxanthum odoratum	sweet vernalgrass
	Bromus pubescens	hairy woodland brome
	Cinna arundinacea	sweet woodreed
	Dactylis glomerata	orchardgrass
	Dichanthelium acuminatum	tapered rosette grass
	Dichanthelium clandestinum	deertongue
	Dichanthelium dichotomum	cypress panicgrass
	Festuca subverticillata	nodding fescue
	Glyceria striata	fowl mannagrass
	Holcus lanatus	common velvetgrass
	Leersia virginica	whitegrass
	Microstegium vimineum	Japanese stiltgrass
	Muhlenbergia sp.	muhly
	Panicum sp.	panicgrass
	Phalaris arundinacea	reed canarygrass
	Poa alsodes	grove bluegrass
	Poa compressa	Canada bluegrass
	Poa trivialis	rough bluegrass
Polemoniaceae	*Phlox stolonifera*	creeping phlox
Polygonaceae	*Polygonum caespitosum*	Oriental ladysthumb
	Polygonum punctatum	dotted smartweed
	Polygonum sagittatum	arrowleaf tearthumb
	Polygonum scandens	climbing false buckwheat
	Polygonum sp.	knotweed
	Polygonum virginianum	jumpseed
	Rumex crispus	curly dock
	Rumex obtusifolius	bitter dock
Primulaceae	*Lysimachia quadrifolia*	whorled yellow loosestrife
Ranunculaceae	*Actaea racemosa*	black baneberry
	Clematis sp.	leather flower
	Clematis virginiana	devil's darning needles
	Ranunculaceae	buttercup
	Ranunculus abortivus	littleleaf buttercup
	Ranunculus hispidus	bristly buttercup
Rosaceae	*Agrimonia gryposepala*	tall hairy agrimony
	Agrimonia parviflora	harvestlice
	Agrimonia sp.	agrimony
	Crataegus sp.	hawthorn
	Duchesnea indica	Indian strawberry
	Fragaria virginiana	Virginia strawberry
	Geum canadense	white avens
	Malus coronaria	sweet crabapple
	Malus sp.	apple
	Potentilla simplex	common cinquefoil
	Potentilla sp.	cinquefoil
	Prunus serotina	black cherry
	Prunus sp.	plum
	Rosa multiflora	multiflora rose

Family	Latin_name	Common
Rosaceae (cont)	*Rubus allegheniensis*	Allegheny blackberry
	Rubus occidentalis	black raspberry
	Rubus sp.	blackberry
Rubiaceae	*Cephalanthus occidentalis*	common buttonbush
	Galium aparine	stickywilly
	Galium asprellum	rough bedstraw
	Galium tinctorium	stiff marsh bedstraw
	Galium triflorum	fragrant bedstraw
	Mitchella repens	partridgeberry
Scrophulariaceae	*Veronica officinalis*	common gypsyweed
	Veronica sp.	speedwell
Simaroubaceae	*Ailanthus altissima*	tree of heaven
Smilacaceae	*Smilax glauca*	cat greenbrier
	Smilax rotundifolia	roundleaf greenbrier
Solanaceae	*Solanum carolinense*	Carolina horsenettle
Thelypteridaceae	*Thelypteris noveboracensis*	New York fern
Ulmaceae	*Celtis occidentalis*	common hackberry
	Ulmus americana	American elm
	Ulmus rubra	slippery elm
	Ulmus sp.	elm
Urticaceae	*Boehmeria cylindrica*	smallspike false nettle
	Laportea canadensis	Canadian woodnettle
	Pilea pumila	Canadian clearweed
Verbenaceae	*Verbena urticifolia*	white vervain
Violaceae	*Viola pubescens*	downy yellow violet
	Viola sororia	common blue violet
	Viola sp.	violet
	Viola striata	striped cream violet
Vitaceae	*Parthenocissus quinquefolia*	Virginia creeper
	Vitis riparia	riverbank grape
	Vitis sp.	grape
	Vitis vulpina	frost grape

NPS 336/101589, 476/101589 March 2010

National Park Service
U.S. Department of the Interior

Natural Resource Program Center
1201 Oakridge Drive, Suite 150
Fort Collins, CO 80525

www.nature.nps.gov

EXPERIENCE YOUR AMERICA ™